Learning Perl 6

JJ Merelo

Contents

1

Introduction

This book is about learning programming using a promising, and almost completely new, language: Perl 6. But it is only Perl 6 specific in a minority of the content. Most chapters that deal with Perl 6 could be rewritten using any other language, preferably a new, cool language such as Go or Rust. I, or someone, might do it some day. But for the time being, let us be content with the Perl 6 content. Which is also new and cool.

You can check out the GitHub repository for this book [https://goo.gl/dgnDD9] . It will also contain evolving versions of new chapters and volumes.

2

Principles

A few principles that inspire this (book|booklet|manual|you name it), originally conceived to help non-programmers get into Perl 6.

Learning should be fun and engaging: learn by doing.

The best way to make people actually learn something is by putting immediately to practice whatever is being learned, be it programming or weaving. So you should have your computer handy and learn the tools as soon as possible to put things to practice.

You are the master of your learning process, and tools, and outcome.

You should learn at your own step, stopping whenever you want and actually taking lessons when you feel like doing it. Engagement will ensue.

Learning never stops.

If you learn only during the short period where *class* is taking place, you will not learn too much. You have to digest and assimilate and come up with new ideas anytime and anywhere. Some of them will be relevant to whatever you are learning, some of them will be revealed as relevant later on, some of them will be simply discarded. But you can leverage whatever experience you have to enhance what you are learning, even more so if it is a programming language.

Learning is a two-way process. There is no professor, no student: learning happens ideally in a community.

This is kinda *zen*, but then the whole thing stinks of a holistic experience, where you learn about life by learning about programming and back. That also means that learning comes from every direction at once: the other students, maybe whoever is preparing objectives and material for the day, but that person will also learn new things about him or herself and about whatever is teaching, because the best way to learn is to prepare something to be taught to others.

Besides, there is no learning outside self-learning. But maybe that is a completely different story.

3

Motivation

This is (mostly) a book on Perl 6. But my initial intention was not to show how to program in Perl 6. Here are a few of my actual motivations, which might also be your own for actually reading and following this book.

Teaching programming to (almost) non-programmers.

Most programming books seem to be written either for people that already know how to program or for people that barely knows how to press keys. There must be a middle ground, and I try to tread it with this book. If know how to use a computer, you should be ready to go the whole nine yards and learn to create things in Perl 6 by the end of the book, if that eventually happens.

Contemplate the possibilities of Perl 6 as a beginner's language.

There seems to be a consensus that there is such a thing as a *good language for beginners*, and that that language is Python. Well, maybe it is, but why would any other languages, Rust, JavaScript or even C++ be worse? Asking about the best programming language for beginners is like asking about the best foreign language for beginners. Evidently, the best is the language you want to learn. If you want to learn Chinese, you do not learn first... whatever language is closer to yours and easier than Chinese (maybe Vietnamese? No idea, really, I got trapped in the metaphor). You learn Chinese and are done with it.

Point is, when you want to learn to program you usually have some kind of job or task in mind. The best language to learn programming is a language that can do that job. And Perl 6 can be that language.

Show the beauty and craft of programming.

"Good technically, but lacks passion" is probably one of the worst things that can be said about a musician or even a footballer. Should be the case also for programmers. Those focused on getting the job done well *technically* will probably lack the will, or the stamina, to learn new things or to completely switch the language or the toolbelt you are using. Along with programming, you have to make students learn the craft and also the beauty of a minimalist, fast and beautiful program.

Make learn by doing

Which boils down to "talk little, do a lot". No slides, no heavyweight course materials, just a screen with examples, and make people perform short tasks and reproduce what is being said by themselves. Hands have better memory than eyes. Use that.

In this book, in most cases activities will have a particular purpose and will follow or flow from one chapter, or asides, to the next ones, so that you will end up building one, or several, scripts or programs or even notes that will be useful by themselves.

4

The tools of the trade

Programming is learned by programming; but in order to actually
make the programs work and do something you have to use programs
that are run from operating systems, in fact *prototyping*; Seen in another way, you are trying to solve a problem for a target audience,
yourself, by choosing the right tools. In this phase you will find that
there is no perfect tool for doing everything.

> Although the combination Linux + Emacs comes pretty
> close

Let's start with the operating system. That would be Linux. Whew,
that was short. Although nowadays Linux is everywhere and you can
have a Linux command line in Windows 10, and of course also in the
Macs. But let's proceed to that thing that actually allows users to run
programs, the *shell*.

Shells

Then, the command line interpreter, also called *shell*. This
might seem like a given, but in fact different command line inter-
preters have different capabilities. In fact, even the humble bash

[https://goo.gl/6RLx3F] has interesting capabilities you can use. Main thing you want to tap is the possibility of displaying interesting information in the command line, such as the directory you are working on or, later on, the branch of the repository you are in. And, in that sense, there are quite a few choices here, but the main thing about them is the possibility of *theming* them, that is, making a configuration that allows, mostly, find the information we mention above by just selecting a *theme*. In that sense zsh [https://goo.gl/WJH6z] and fish [https://goo.gl/rtNNRi] are very strong contenders. Install them the usual way, and then select a theme that goes easily with your programming habits; Oh My Zsh [https://goo.gl/vETZQ] or bash-it [https://goo.gl/c5ZKrj] are good places to start.

Play a bit with the themes or options until you find one with all the colors and contrast you want. And then come back here for the...

Editors.

The choice of an editor goes beyond mere utility to become an identity, a side to stand when the flame war starts. As above, the motto is always *suit yourself*, but since we are in the realm of Perl6, I would propose Atom [https://goo.gl/GOgVPE] as the editor to use. It is a modern editor, it has got a good and evolving support for Perl 6, and it is free software. Perl6 scripts look positively pretty [https://goo.gl/LYqp83] with the Atom Perl 6 support, and they include goodies such as completing variable names and that kind of things. However, Emacs goes a bit further providing an environment where you can work with all kind of Unicode characters, run the REPL and complete variables if you so like.

You can also run chunks of code with the script plugin installed [https://goo.gl/54Wnzb] . However, for the time being we are going to focus on expressions, and these will not print anything except from the REPL. You can keep it for later if you so wish.

Not that the traditional Emacs and Vi/Vim are not good choices too. At least Emacs, but Atom is easier to use and is improving in speed and support by the minute. Besides, it has got everything it takes for professional editor: syntax highlighting, being able to do some checks from the editor itself, and allow running and debugging. It has got all that, so that will be it.

To go with the editor, you need some relatively fast way of inputting some characters such as   or . I have used the application "Character Map" that comes with Ubuntu; after finding a character by the name of the alphabet, you can go to Character Details and copy/paste it to wherever you want it used. You can also click twice and the character will appear in the "Text to copy" slot.

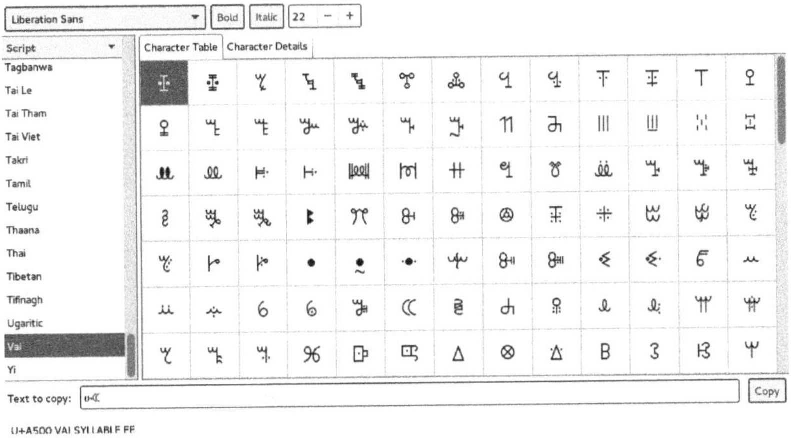

Figure 4.1: Character map for Unicode

However, if you are an old-timer getting into new languages, probably emacs will be much more suitable for you. Although the mode that supports perl6 is in flux at this precise moment [https://goo.gl/zkdpjb] it does have a couple of advantages that set it apart: the integrated shell that allows you to work easily with code alongside REPL, and also how easy it is to input Unicode characters. Which are not necessary for Perl6, but are terribly convenient.

Of course, something would be missing here if I did not mention 'vim'. Here you go, a mention.

Shells within editors

Editors are cool because they allow to work with all kind of symbols
that are not exactly text, or that cannot be produced with a combination of key strokes. Emacs is great at that, and it can access the
whole set of symbols that are out there by name using a combination
of keys. And it can also run a shell inside, your favorite shell, in fact.
So enter `emacs` and then type `Escape key + x` and then, when a prompt
appears in the lower line, `shell` and you will have your shell running
inside Emacs, with access to all kind of goodies, like saving sessions as
files, searching using all Emacs facilities, and all kind of symbols that
can be used in it.

5

We need to talk about Unicode

This section, along with some other you will find interleaved with the Perl 6 ones, does not belong to the language proper, but it is still something that has to be mentioned. Languages are used to write applications, and these can use any language in the world. Unicode [https://goo.gl/UMAuiW] is the way to use any alphabet, and some neographies [https://goo.gl/j8DOBY] and emoticons, in our programs. Luckily enough, Perl6 packs one of the best supports for this; unluckily, Unicode is complicated *per se*, so we will have to learn a bit of linguistics to understand how we, later on, are going to handle this, which we will even if we write only for ourselves.

First important concept is the *codepoint*. A code point is pretty much equivalent to a letter, although it can be a symbol or also a formatting instruction such as Tab or Newline. Every code point corresponds to a numeric combination, which is usually expressed in hexadecimal; for instance, `0x2017` corresponds to the character ‗, part of a table-drawing set. Every character also has a series of attributes, including the category; this character belongs to the `Po` category [https://goo.gl/i2hNeH] , meaning that it is *Punctuation, other*. The properties [https://goo.gl/3YcgAA] include a series of attributes such as the fact that they are numeric or can do things like folding to a particular case or be joined to the next character, or even if the direction they are written in.

Characters are written as graphemes [https://goo.gl/JxHkUE] , and usually a code point corresponds to a single written grapheme; however, in some cases code points group to form a *grapheme cluster*, which is a set of code points that constitute a grapheme; the most common example is letters with marks such as á, but more complicated expressions might be thought of. Or not, depending on your imagination.

You write graphemes and grapheme clusters as *glyphs*, or letters. And these are typeset, in a particular environment, using *fonts*. A font is a set of mathematical formulae, yes, there is math involved, that allows to render a particular letter in many different sizes and forms such as italics or boldface. The fact that they are a formula, and that you have to design formulae for every single glyph, means that not all glyphs might be available in all fonts. Some fonts will have all, or most of them, some of them not. And that, in turn, means that some Etruscan letter such as this one   that renders beautifully in your editor might show up as an x-marked rectangle or question mark somewhere else, a console or a word processor. In fact, depending on how you are reading this, you might not see the glyph I'm referring to at all. Some other glyphs, like this jack of diamonds , will not show up on your editor or even in a PDF document. However, you will be able to see it in most browsers.

Your take away message here should that you need to know how to use Unicode in whatever program you use, and that some particular structures of the program, like operators or names, will use graphemes with particular properties, probably something alphabetic-like. Also that Unicode is complicated, but that you should better learn about it as soon as possible, as in now.

6

The expressions

The first thing you need to know about a language, any language, is how to compute things. Compute in the more general sense: combine things to give other things. This, in general, is called expression, which, also in general, is a bunch of symbols linked by **operators**.

Generally, modern computer languages are able to work with many different kind of symbols, and Perl6 is no exception. Let's start with that.

REPLs and how to use them as glorified calculators

A REPL [https://goo.gl/4bxFP] is a Read-Eval-Print loop. it is a program included with most interpreted languages, that presents a command-line prompt and into which you can type expressions, and, later on, full statements. But, for the time being, let's type

```
perl6
```

And we will be into a perl6 REPL into which you can type Perl6 stuff.

Let's try the simplest thing:

```
To exit type 'exit' or '^D'
> sin(π/2)
```

You will have to find a way to type that , by copy/pasting it from some website or Google or right from here. It will return the sine of /2, which, as you know, is 1.

And this is cool, because only some languages are able to handle this kind of expressions, and, even more, to use it correctly in math. But you can do even more:

```
sin(π/2) +1
```

You can do that by copying/pasting, or else install Linenoise, a command line that allows you to go back to previous command by typing arrow-up. Do it with

```
zef install Linenoise
```

You can use the usual arithmetic operators +,-,*,/ but Perl6 adds two typographic operators, ÷ and × (these ones are produced in the Spanish keyboard with May+AltGr+ comma or period), like

```
sin(π/3) × sin(π/3) + cos(π/3) × cos(π/3)
```

Or, even better

```
sin(π/3)² + cos(π/3)²
```

One of the objectives of Perl6 is to use the whole range of characters that Unicode, if not modern keyboards, offer. This simplifies expressions and makes them more readable.

You will not find all numbers in superscript mode. If you want to raise a number to the /x/th power, use **.

```
3**25
```

Arithmetic only takes you so far in programming. We will learn how to deal, and operate, with all kinds of data in this glorified calculator.

Now that we mention Unicode

Unicode is the way to express all alphabets in the world, and then some things that are not really alphabets. It uses up to around sixty thousand symbols, and allows us to write, using modern operating systems, editors and languages, anything that would have to be expressed in living or dead languages, and even some emoticons. Unicode is evolving constantly, and for the people means that they will be able to use characters that are usual in their own language, and also some usual in mathematical expressions.

Since not all languages, editors, operating systems or even keyboards are **modern** in that sense, some impedance should be expected. But Perl 6 will not get in your way, allowing you to use them just they way they should, so if you want to raise something to the second power you will not have to, although you can, write x**2 but simply x^2.

It's not only numbers

All the expressions written above are numbers.

```
(sin(π/3)² + cos(π/3)²).^name
```

is going to return `Num`, indicating that it is simply a Number, actually a real number. This dot .. together with surrounding the expression via parentheses that group what is inside them, evaluating them, is a way to apply a *property* or to call a *method* on that object. In Perl6, everything is an object, and objects have a class, and you want to call methods that correspond to objects of that class, append a dot and use the method, possibly with some arguments like `method(in, "my", $madness)`. Let's not worry about that for the time being, or about classes themselves, or for that matter, about the caret `^`.

> Which is actually calling a meta-class method [https://goo.gl/YNvTYL] . Powerful stuff. But for the time being `^name` returns a string with the name of the class and that's that.

Just with the fact that every expression is an object, and those objects belong to a class; every class in Perl6 *descends* from the ur-class called or Mu. And among the properties of Mu [https://goo.gl/rqPEY5] is that you can call this `^name`. Any other class descends from this one, so *you can call .`^name` on any object of any class.* That is the take-home message, even if you might not know, so far, what is an object, or a class. Second take home message: *different objects also have different classes.*

Since both *objects* at the sides of the + are Nums, you can add or subtract them or do any other arithmetic operation, but you cannot do

```
sin(π/3)² + cos(π/3)² + " is 1"
```

will yield this error

Figure 6.1: Errored expression in the REPL

And the reason for that can be found out by typing:

```
" is 1".^name
```

Which, whatever it is, is not a Num, so it cannot be added. That shows that there are more types of data you can use and work with from the REPL. In fact, there are a lot. In general, you cannot mix and match and, also in general, every one has got its own operators you can work with. You can mix fractions with integer numbers, for instance:

```
⅓+4/3
```

And

```
(⅓+4/3).^name
```

will return Rat, a the class used for rational numbers, same as ⅓+4. In fact, most floating point numbers in Perl 6 will be represented as rational [https://goo.gl/dJFkFW] , unless we explicitly tell the interpreter to deal with them as floating point, that is real, numbers, which,

BTW, cannot be something else that fractional numbers since they use a finite representation in computers. Mostly.

However, in some cases you can try and mix different things using an operator. Operator "~" concatenates stuff, that is, joins things that look like words and letters, for instance

```
6 ~ "6"
```

will return 66, and anything you put there will be concatenated. ~ is an operator that is not picky about what it has got in both ends.

You cannot add strings together, because that is what they are, but curiously enough, you can multiply them:

```
"1" ~ "\n" ~ "2" x 2 ~ "\n" ~ "3" x 3 ~ "\n" ~ "2" x 2\
  ~ "\n" ~ "1"
```

This being a rather nice and utterly useless example on the operator x, which *multiplies* or rather *replicates* whatever character of string it is related to. Introduced together with \n, the carriage return, so that if forms a nice pile of stuff.

Which is shorter and better in this example

```
for <1 2 3 2 1>  { say $_ x $_ }
```

but that's something we will see later on, when we talk about loops and all that's nice and beautiful about it.

Lists of things are also game.

Numbers and words are simple things. But you can string them together in something more complex. You can have groups of them, or lists of them, or combine them as sets of lists of sets of whatever. Perl 6 is great because you do not need to make all things in a complex structure be of the same type. You can create a list with the less than and more than sign, this way:

```
<a b 7 ⅓ π²>
```

And with lists, you can do things like sorting:

```
sort <a b 7 ⅓ π²>
```

or combine lists to create a new one using the X operator, called **cross product**

```
<a b 7 ⅓ π²> X < → ← >
```

You can also combine in some other ways, adding one list to another.

```
<a b 7 ⅓ π²> , < → ← >
```

The simple *comma* operator is going to create a new list with two elements, each one of which is a list. You can **flatten** it:

```
flat <a b 7 ⅓ π²> , < → ← >
```

You can already do interesting things with these lists (or arrays, or vectors, stuff in a row, whatever). For instance, you want to pick one element randomly,

```
(flat <a b 7 ⅓ π²> , < → ← >).pick
```

will return, every time you run it, a different element. You can do that as many times as you want, but it is much easier to use roll to do it many times for you.

```
< → ← >.roll(6)
```

will return a whole quiver of arrows.

Maybe you want a single element of the array:

```
< → ← >.roll(6)[3]
```

This will return the 4th element, taking into account that all arrays start with 0. Otherwise known as a random arrow. Or you might want to extract a range

```
(flat <a b 7 ⅓ π²> , < → ← >)[3..6]
```

uses the *range* operator .. (that is, two points), which generates a contiguous sequence of elements. Otherwise known as, well, range. But these ranges also behave as arrays:

```
(0..10)[3..6]
```

although they are not exactly the same:

```
(0..10).^name
```

will, effectively, return `Range`.

This is just the start of complex structures with Perl. More to come in the next chapters.

7

Thinking like computers do

You probably know, or at least have made an educated guess, that computers are unlike humans. But since expressions are entered in pretty much the same way you would use somewhere else, it's no big deal. However, once you want to deconstruct what actually needs to be done to make a computer do whatever you want it to do, you have to start to think like a computer, in what is known as computational thinking. It is kind of a game of "Simon says". You have to precede every instruction you give a computer by something that indicates you want it to do precisely that, and then you have to say very precisely what it needs to do.

But there is more to that, the fact that you also need to indicate the *sequence* of actions you want the computer to do by indicating that in your program. When you work with the REPL, as we have done above, the sequence is quite clear: you say something, press Enter, the computer thinks for a while or what looks like nothing, you have the response. However, when the program gets a bit more complicated, you also have to think, in a particular point in time, where the computer might be and what that implies regarding values or results you need to proceed.

Which is why we talk about computational thinking [https://goo.gl/i1huQ] as a series of techniques for solving problems using computers, including all the steps you need to take to identify the problem, put it in a way that can be understood and processed by a computer, and then express every step as instructions in program that will, eventually, solve the problem.

We will get back to this later on, but for the time being there are a couple of techniques you will need to understand. First is *pattern recognition*, which means finding what several different pieces of information have in common and, in turn, what to do to solve a problem in a case given that you know how to solve it in another case which follows the same pattern. When you find something that has a regular increasing or arithmetic pattern, for instance, you will discover that you can use lists or sequences to solve it, and apply whatever you know already on how to deal with sequences.

The second technique we should focus on right now is *problem decomposition*, how to break down a problem in different parts that can, more easily, solved. For instance, you want to find what would be the number a sequence will reach if left to grow until infinity; first you will have to solve the problem of representing the sequence, which might not be immediate, and then how to apply known techniques of limit finding, such as finding the function that represents the sequence [https://goo.gl/YDyN17] and then applying what is known about function limits to that sequence.

Every part of a problem will eventually become an instruction or group of instructions called usually *subroutines* or *functions*. But for the time being, it is enough to know that breaking down a problem in parts you already know how to solve is the key for solving problems of any size.

8

To infinity and beyond

If you know in advance every single term of a list, writing them down as above is the way to handle them. However, you might know a few terms of the lists, or how they are generated, and that is that. Let us see how to deal with them in Perl 6

Working with ranges and sequences

For long lists, you might want to use only the first and last term

```
1...222
```

via the **yada, yada, yada** operator, or, even better,

```
1 … 333
```

But the coolest thing with lists is the stuff you can do to all of them at the same time:

```
[+] 1 … 333
```

will add everything together. Any operator you put inside brackets will be applied to all in turn. Try [*] 1 … 333, for instance.

But the coolness factor can be increased:

```
[+] 1,3 … 333
```

and even

```
[+] 1,3,9 … 333
```

The [] is called a *reduce* operation. If you have heard some big data buzz, you have probably heard about an operation called **map/reduce**. Well, this is the *reduce* part. And it is so easy to do with Perl6.

Because Perl6 is able to deal with arithmetic and geometric progressions out of the box. And even infinite ones:

```
1,3,9 … ∞
```

You can obtain the 100th term using

```
(1,3,9 … ∞)[100]
```

or, why not, the terms from 1000 to 1100

```
(1,3,9 … ∞)[1000…1100]
```

which will return a pile of numbers, separated by spaces. It is quite usual to start from 0 and go to a particular number. The *caret* = ^ = is used to indicate *0 to* the number that follows it

```
(0,5,10 … ∞)[^25]
```

will list the 25 first elements of the list of multiples of 5.

Besides, at the same time, we have seen how to deal with a single term in a list, and how to work with a series of terms. You can use infinite syntax to generate also finite lists if you do not want to compute in advance the precise terms of it. For example, above you will be working on the 1000th term and on of an infinite list, without working out if it is exactly 3000 or some such. You can check out this Advent calendar entry for a few samples of Perl6 coolness too [https://goo.gl/TrHNdD]

Operating on lists

Lists are perfectly good subjects for this calculator on steroids we have in the REPL. Whatever combination you think about, it is probably possible to do it on lists; some of them will work also on infinite lists, but most probably not. We have already seen [+] work on a list of numbers. Any sensible operation like [*] will also work. But this will also yield a result:

[~] 'a'..'z'

collating together all elements in the alphabet. Preceding it with \. which you can think of as an accumulator, will instead create another array whose elements are the accumulation of the operation up to that element. Better if you try it:

[\~] 'a'..'z'

This can be very useful when working on accumulative series, for instance, what is the sequence of factorials up to 25?

[*] 1..25

This accumulator is called a *zip* operator. We will see later on what it actually means, for the time being it just makes operating with series a bit easier.

But single lists only take you so far. Previously we have seen the comma for kind-of joining two lists. But there are multiple ways of creating new lists by combining them. For instance, the *cross* operator X will create a list of lists from two of them

(1,3...10) X (2,4...10)

will combine all even and odd numbers in pairs, combining 1 with 2 to 10, then doing the same with 3... This can be useful if you want to create a combination, but even more so if you turn X into a hyper-operator by using it to precede any operation such as *

(1,3...10) X* (2,4...10)

will create a *flat* list with the results of multiplying the pairs we have generated before. This can be useful for complicated arithmetics, but sometimes we only want to pair a couple of lists to create a new one that takes one element from each one, combining them like the tooth of a zipper. This operation is appropriately named Zip and represented by Z

```
(5,10...Inf)[^20] Z (4,8...Inf)[^20]
```

This creates a new list that zips together similar terms in the sequence of multiples of 4 and 5. Can we multiply them to create a succession of multiples of 20? Maybe...

```
(5,10...Inf)[^20] Z* (4,8...Inf)[^20]
```

Doing stuff to lists

Well, that is precisely what we have been doing above. But we need to do more. A lot more.

All we have been doing is combining lists with each other. We have also been using lists of exactly the same length. But we might need to do some basic operation to a list, or create one list that is not exactly an arithmetic or geometric progression. For instance, this

```
(1/2,1/3...Inf)[5]
```

will not do what you expect it to do, which would be 1/5. Writing the whole range

```
(1/2,1/3...Inf)[^5]
```

will show that, what it is actually doing is to turn it into an arithmetic sequence that subtracts 0.166667 from the previous one, despite being relatively clear, for a human, that we are trying to create the 1/n. Succession. We can do that, however, using the hyperoperators `<<>>` and derived. Check this out

```
1 <</<< (1..100)
```

will return precisely what we are looking for, a descending sequence of numbers that ends with 0.01. Please note that we can no longer use an infinite (lazy) sequence: we have to be concrete.

This `<</<<` is known as an *hyperoperator*, because it takes a humble operator like `/` and turns it into a machine that deals with lists. It can also be written «/« with the direction of the angular brackets pointing at the *smaller* thing, in this case a single number vs. a list.

What happens if you do

```
<1 2> <</<< (1..100)
```

is kind of funny. It is like applying the cookie cutter in the left hand side to the right hand side: the first element will be divided by 1, the second by 2, and so on... You can even take one wing << from the hyperdrive, and use it to, for instance, negate a sequence:

```
-<< (1..100)
```

When the two lists have the same length, the arrows can go in any direction, it will not matter much. Let us create random fixtures for a (subset of) the Premier League

```
( <ARS AST BOU CHE EVE LEI LIV MCI MUN NEW>.pick(10)
    «~»
( " - " «~« <ARS AST BOU CHE EVE LEI LIV MCI MUN\
  NEW>.pick(10)))
    »~» "\n"
```

This, which could admittedly be a little shorter, uses these hyperoperators to combine acronyms so that they are separated by a dash, which is what = " - " «~« = does, and then put the whole result in different lines, which is done by the = »~» \n = in the last line. A great achievement, with a small amount of coding involved. We are using throughout the ~ string concatenation operator, which is what allows us to create such a compact statement.

9

Working as a team

You will never walk alone when solving a problem using computers. Even if you are working in a side project, something you thought about yourself, you will need an easy way to keep track of changes and also to easily incorporate whatever suggestions or even changes somebody else might be doing to your code. And that easy way is to use git [https://goo.gl/k6TRGo] . git is described as a distributed source code manager, but it is much more than that, it is a way of life. git organizes code in *repositories*, pretty much corresponding to projects, but including also artifacts such as documentation, manuals and examples.

As a way of life, it needs much more than a single section in a book. You will eventually learn as you go, but for the purpose of this, let us say you have opened an account in an online Git server such as GitHub [https://goo.gl/KkZ8] . GitHub is free for public repositories, and even for a few closed ones if you are a student. If you do not feel comfortable with this, do not worry, you can use BitBucket [https://goo.gl/Ua98O] , which allows private repositories with some limitations on the number of users and number of repos.

Be that as it may, you will need a repository to store all the files that you will be writing in this, maybe also your course notes. It is going to be fun start to create a single program, and keep changing it over the same file; git will record changes and you will be able to track your own progress over this file. In order to do that, create a repository or project in any of them, and choose a sensible free software license, as well as Perl as a language (closest to Perl6) and also generate a `README.md`, which is in Markdown.

That creates a git repository in whatever computer hosts GitHub (or BitBucket), but git is a distributed system, and you can synchronize your computer with the contents of the repository out there. Bring it down with

`git clone https://github.com/yourname/yourrepo`

and please note I am using `https` here. You can also, and in fact should, use the *ssh* address, which will be something like `git@github.com:yourname/yourrepo.git` and in fact you should, but for the time being let us let it be. Remember to take down the username and password you have used, because you will need later on.

That command will create a `yourrepo` directory hanging from wherever you are. Change to it with `cd yourrepo` and start working there. For instance, create a new file with `touch a_new_file`. Not everything in the directory is *in* the repository, you have to purposefully add to it.

`git add a_new_file`

This only tells the repository it should be aware of the file. But then you have to actually do something about it, like telling the repo you are happy with the file such as it is and it should be registered, or *committed.* You should go:

`git commit -m "Adds file for doing stuff"`

You are not done yet. All these changes are local. You can continue adding things

10

Thinking logically

In many cases you are going to need to check whether something is true or false: check if a file exists, check if a number is bigger or smaller than another, or even check if a complicated logical proposition is true or not. In fact, everything in computers uses logic, to the point that all information is codified using true or false values; a single true/false value is called a *bit*. There are so many layers over that single bit that you do not need to be much concerned about them, but you need to know about expressing and using logic in programs, and specially in Perl 6, because computing is all about taking decisions, doing this or that depending on something else. That is what we will deal with right next.

The truth is...

"Out there". "I am your father". All of these things together. Well, truth is True and false is False in Perl6. However, there are other things that are also true, or not, depending on the context, because, as we have seen before, the types and thus the real value of things flow and change depending on the context. Fortunately, we have a handy operator that asks any and everything if it is true or not: ?.

So let's see what kind of things are true or not:

```
?<< ("","False",0,1,333,0.5)
```

will show us two `False=s`; the `""` and the `0`. So empty strings and void numbers are equivalent to false. Also empty arrays, check out `=?()`, while non-empty arrays are `True`. Besides, we are using here, similarly to what we used before, a single operator applied to all the elements in a list, which we surround with parentheses and sprinkle with commas since they are of different types: strings and numbers... This operator will apply, to every single member of the list, the *unary* operation `?`. That is akin to doing `?""` and so on, until the end of the list. Perl6 saves typing and frees us from metacarpal tunnel syndrome.

And what you can ask, you can negate:

```
!<< ("","False",0,1,333,0.5)
```

will result exactly in the opposite. `!` negates the expression it is in front of. By the way, these operators that are *in front of* are called prefix operators; since they operate in a single element they are also *unary*, but that goes without saying if they are prefixing something. Operators in the middle of two things are called *infix* and they happen to be *binary*. Finally, there is also a *ternary* operator, but we will get to that soon.

So, finally, `?True` is `True` and `!True` is `False`. And there is no bigger true than that. So

```
so "this"
```

is `True` and

```
so ""
```

is, obviously, `False`.

Comparing things

Affirming and negating is a great way to learn philosophy, but we need a bit of arithmetic too. Let's see how Perl6 performs simple comparison operations

`3 > 2`

will return `True`,

`2 == 3`

will return `False`, because 2 is not equal (=) to 3. Remember, = is used for comparison, and the rest of the operators are quite usual. Whenever an operations can be true or not, it will return a `False` or `True` value, and all these comparison operations are. This equality operator is quite smart

`2 == 3`

will return `False`, but

`2 == "2"`

will return `True`. The *smartness* of the operation means that it will be able to recognize something even across different types, as in this case, where we are comparing a number (or `Int`) with a `Str`. It is even smarter

`3 == III`

because it understands, as in this case, Roman numerals.

There is also ~~, which is kind of an universal matching, equivalent to *is a kind of.* It behaves as == when the type is the same, although

`3 ~~ "3.0"`

will return `False`. = 3 ~~ Int , however, will be =True.

All these equality operators have a dark side which does exactly the opposite. We have seen before that ! is the negation of all that's True, so, effectively, != will mean *not equal* and !~ *does not match.* Check it out, it is really true. That it is that way, I mean.

In case you are working with strings, > is not going to work, with "a" < "b" yielding an error that tells you it cannot convert a string to a number; it will work, though, for "10" < "011", but after turning them into numbers; alphabetically, "011" goes *before* "10". That is why there are specific operators for strings, whose names are built as acronyms of the operation, for instance, `ge` for *greater than or equal*, as in

```
"aardvark" ge "bee"
```

This will take into account the lexicographical order, which is kind of like the alphabetical, but taking into account ordering in Unicode. Thus

```
"ρ" le "P"
```

because apparently small letters go *after* capital letters, but

```
"🂡" gt "ش"
```

because, well, that is the way it is.

And filtering them

(Also applying things to a whole lot of them). Now that we know how to deal with truths and untruths, we can use this knowledge to deal with sequences and filter them depending on whether a condition is true or not. We can, for instance, use ready-made functions such as is-prime

```
(2000..2100).grep( { .is-prime} )
```

As you might remember, putting parentheses around an expression, in this case a Range (remember, two periods) turns it into an *object* and thus something that is amenable of using some methods. grep [https://goo.gl/BmJkQn] is one of them: given a list, applies an expression to every member of the list returning another list with only the elements where the expression is true. The expression which is surrounded by curly braces, as you see, is between parentheses, and since every element is treated as an object by itself by grep, the .is-prime way of writing it indicates that you are taking the first element, applying the is-prime function, select that element for the result if it is true, and so no. That expression above tells us the number of prime years (not premium years) in this century. How many are there?

What there is is many ways of writing that. To reduce clutter, Perl6 allows also the parentheses to be suppressed.

```
(2000..2100).grep: { .is-prime}
```

by a colon. And you can also invert the way of dealing with this, putting grep at the forefront

```
grep { .is-prime}, 1..Inf
```

and, right there, you have the list of all prime numbers. Which one is the number 1000th? (it might take a while).

In fact, if you are applying a single method that takes only one parameter, such as the one above to every element, there is an even simpler way of doing it [https://goo.gl/4u5VQi] :

```
(0,π/2,π,3*π/2,2*π)».sin
```

Using the parentheses and commas we create an array, and the ». construction will apply the operation behind to each and every member of it, returning the sine of all these angles. Any operation with a single operand you can think of can be applied, in this way, to a whole array of things. Which is cool. Even cooler, you can use the so we learned above to filter only those whose cosine is not zero:

```
grep { .so }, (0,π/2,π,3*π/2,2*π)».cos
```

This might work with precision in the future, but for the time being the result of cos is pretty close to 0, but not exactly so, which means that grep actually returns all elements of the array, which are effectively non-zero.

You might want to do simpler things to arrays, like finding the minimum:

```
min (3/4, 5/6, 3/8, 2/3)
```

. From this, you can figure out how to find the maximum, right? And even the greatest common denominator and least common multiple, as long as the array is populated only by integers.

```
[lcm] (5, 77, 343)
```

And we are doing some trick here, using square brackets to turn an operator, lcm, which applies to only two operands, to one that can be applied to a whole array. You can do the same with any operator. Give it a try. In fact we did it way before, when we wanted to concatenate a list. Do you remember?

```
[~] 'a'..'z'
```

Well, this is pretty much the same and rather not what I intended for this chapter initially, but you get carried away and this is what happens. That chapter also mentioned the *accumulator* \. You can put it to good use here:

```
[\lcm] (5, 77, 343, 881)
```

computing the accumulated least common multiple for one, two and up the the four elements of the array.

Besides doing thing with arrays, you can also do things with, well, other things, and arrays. For instance, computing whether an element is or not in a particular array,

```
332 ∈ (7,14...2000)
```

using ∈, which is the mathematical symbol for *belongs to* and returns False in this case. That can be an easy and straightforward way of finding out multiples, for instance, or if an element is included in a more complex sequence.

Multiples that you can also extract using grep [https://goo.gl/rjS4PF]

```
(1..100).grep(* %% 7)
```

where, in this case, * is a stand-in for the element in the list, which we had not used before in this way; we had used it before as the end of a sequence meaning *everything*. This is pretty much the same, *everyone*. Perl6 reuses symbols like this in different contexts, but at the same time it gives them similar, or the same, meaning. That is good and well and saves you from learning lots of different squiggles for stuff that pretty much does the same.

What happens if you want to filter by types? This will do the trick:

```
(¾, π,{ $^p + 7},"a", "b").grep( {$^p.^name ~~ Str} )
```

Since ~~ is the *is a kind of* operator, this expression will return only those things that are *a kind of* String. Which one will those be? Well...

This and that. Or that.

Checks on a list pile up to form a pyramid in which whatever emerges as true or false at the top depends on what happens at the bottom. Sometimes it is enough with one of the conditions holding, sometimes you need all the conditions to hold at the same time. These are the logical operators, which are called AND and OR. ANDing two premises holds true only if both are true, ORing them is true as long as one of them is.

```
(7 > 1) && (7 < 10)
```

is True since both inequalities hold; also

```
True || (7 < 10)
```

is True.

But what happens if we want to do something when an expression is true, and something different when it is false? Could we put all that in an expression. Well, yes:

```
(3 > 2)??"Bigger"!!"Smaller"
```

The ternary operator is one of the few that deals with three arguments. The first one, before the ??, is an expression that can be true or false, or, actually, any of the equivalents we have seen above. If it is true, then the result will be what is between the ?? and the "!!". If it is not, then what is left, what we find behind the !!. What will it be in this case? Check it out and you will see.

This operator is quite useful, and fast, when you want to check alternatives in a single sentence. For instance, checking types

```
("3".^name ~~ (Str))??"Tres"!!3
```

This will return Tres, since "3" is actually a string. Remember that you have to use the parentheses to wrap around the expression, almost always.

You will find these expressions later on in many places. It is worth the while to devote a while to test them so that you end up knowing perfectly how they work and what to do with them.

Back to infinity. And beyond.

Now that we got the hang of expressions we can go back again to these infinite sequences we are so fond of. What we have seen so far are sequences that are either infinite and thus ended with * or ∞ or finite ending with a particular number. But we know now how to add conditions, right? Let's use them in definition of sequences.

```
11,22 ...  * %% 7
```

Where before we had the asterisk or Whatever, now we have a *condition*. When True, the sequence will end. In this case, when it arrives to 77. Maybe we want it to end right before that, in which case we use the *up to, but not including* operator, the dots plus a caret

```
2100,2200 ...^ * %% 400
```

Will yield the years ending a century, in this millennium, that are not [https://goo.gl/5y6iKT] a leap year, since only those that can be divided by 400 actually are leap year.

This is but a simple example, but it allows you to see the flexibility of the language and how some types of expression, logical expressions, can be applied to other part, defining sequences.

11

The command line

In the principle was the command line.

That is so true. You run scripts from the command line, and you go back to it when you are done. But also the Linux was created with a set of command line tools that can be integrated with your program to save you typing and thinking and energy. There is so much you can do with it, that we will need to know how it works, starting with organization of the disk drive.

The disk drive is nowadays mostly solid-state, or else it is so fast you do not need to worry about it. Anyway it is organized like an inverted tree, with the `root` at / and all branches and leaves hanging from it. That tree would branch on *directories* or *folders* and the leaves hanging at the far end would be *files*. In Linux, branching is marked by /, so a file *this.is.a.file* in a folder called *jj* which is inside another folder called *home* will be completely qualified by `/home/jj/this.is.a.file`, or, sometimes, using web-style universal resource identifier, `file://home/jj/this.is.a.file`. The characters beyond the last period are usually called the *extension*. They are no big deal, actually, just a part of the name, but they usually have a conventional value for particular kind of files, like `.txt` for text files and things like that.

When you are working from the command line, you are always in a particular directory, which is called the *working* directory. You probably have used Bash it [https://goo.gl/c5ZKrj] or something like that to show it on the command line; if you have not, well, do it now. cd is used to change this working directory, and you can use absolute names or abbreviations like .. for the directory that contains your current working directory.

We have already seen a few things the operating system can do, including the command *shell*, or command interpreter, which includes some orders and also fetches program for you to run, and also editors. But there are a few more orders that will be invaluable when using Linux as a programmer.

Calling names

Sometimes you need to refer to lots of things at the same time, like a bunch of files with a common characteristic or simply all of them. Linux, in the same way as all modern operating systems, has a way of using *wildcard* characters to mean "lots of things". The most widely used is the *asterisk* *, also the Kleene star for some obscure reason. Anyway, when you find * in an expression it means *whatever*. As in ls * means *list whatever stuff is in this directory* or ls ../* means *list whatever stuff is in the directory right above this one*.

You can combine it with other characters. a*.p6 will mean all files whose name starts with a and has the .p6 *extension*, since whatever goes beyond the last dot is usually called *extension* and usually is peculiar to a kind of files, such as the Perl 6 files in this case.

There are more powerful wildcards [https://goo.gl/PhOk] and many ways of including and excluding particular files. It will help you to know them, but for the time being this wildcard characters is all you need.

Moving stuff around

cp, as in "copy" copies files to another directory, maybe with another name

```
cp this.is.the.original.file ../to/this.is.a.copy
```

will copy the original file to a directory called to, and with a different name. .. is the upper directory. Similarly,

```
mv this.is.the.original.file ../to/this.is.a.copy
```

will *move* or change the name of the file, that is, copy and also remove the original file. If you just want to get rid of a file rm file will do it.

find

Used to find files by name, it is invaluable when you do not remember exactly where you downloaded your repo or you want to find an example of a file you have already done in the past. For instance, typing this in the command line

```
find /home/thisisme -name "*.pl6" -print
```

will return all files with the extension pl6, which is the usual one in Perl6, in your home directory, as long as your username is thisisme; change it to your username to apply it to your particular situation.

find is, then, kind of like ls on steroids. ls will return the files in your folder, or if you do ls -alt will return them sorted by date, which is useful when you do not remember the last file you were working with. It happens.

grep

You do not remember in which particular file you used a name like foo? grep to the rescue

```
grep foo *.pl6
```

will look for your `foo` in all files with the extension `c`.

Creating and destroying things

`mkdir` creates directories, `mkdir -p this/is/a/deep/directory` creates a *leaf* directory and all the rest, and `touch` creates empty files.

You can also use the so called *redirections* to create files from the output of other things. For instance

```
ls *.pl6 > all-perl6-files.txt
```

will create a file that contains the names of all files with that extension, check out the use of the wildcard * discussed just above, while

```
touch I_am_touched
```

creates an empty file. Which, by the way, can be incredibly useful things. If the file is created, it is *touched* in such a way that it is as good as new and will appear first when you list the directory with 'ls -alt', which is the way all directories should be shown.

Finally, here is something that you should use sparingly, if ever. `rm -rf stuff` will delete the directory subtree that starts with `stuff`. And once things have been deleted, they are deleted for ever in Linux. So be careful, and always backup.

12

Pack all your troubles in a bag. And a set.

Perl6 is, intentionally, designed for math, so it includes some representation for data that can be found usually in math courses. Not only that, it can work with them just in the way you did in your school math class, using the same symbols. For instance, let's talk about Sets. And later, we will talk about the type that gives some sense to this chapter's title: *Bags*.

What is a set and what can it do for me.

A set is a group of things whose order does not matter much.

```
set(1,⅓,"foo",{ $^þ %% 3})
```

An *element* of a set can be anything. In this case, we have numbers, strings and a function. Superficially, or at least in the way you define it, it is similar to an array, with the parentheses and all, but it *does* need the word set before it.

```
set(⅓,¼,"a","what?") == set("a","what?",⅓,¼)
```

will return `True` because they define exactly the same set; remember that $==$ was used to check if two things were equal.

In fact, you can easily turn an array into a set, as long as it is an array representing finitely many things and not an infinite one.

```
set(^1000})
```

will create a set with 1000 elements, since `^1000` returns a range with numbers from 0 to 1000.

Sets can be used to represent baskets, or shelves, or groups of people... When order does not make a logical sense, and you are more interested in knowing if something belongs to a set or not, `Set` is the kind of structure you must give your data. For instance, this set would represent the Scottish Premiership for 2016-2017:

```
set( <ABE CEL DUN HAM HEA INV KIL MOT PAR RAN ROS STJ> )
```

where we use the `<>` notation to make shorter the defined array that is later turned into a set. If we compare it to the premiership of the previous year there are subtle changes

```
set( <ABE CEL DUN DUU HAM HEA INV KIL MOT PAR ROS STJ> )
```

, two are in and two out; which ones can be immediately revealed using set operators [https://goo.gl/WLNdFA] :

```
set( <ABE CEL DUN HAM HEA INV KIL MOT PAR RAN ROS STJ> ) ∩
set( <ABE CEL DUN DUU HAM HEA INV KIL MOT PAR ROS STJ> )
```

which returns the set of 11 teams that have not either been promoted or relegated. We can even go ahead and create a list or array of teams in every division

```
(set( <ABE CEL DUN HAM HEA INV KIL MOT PAR RAN ROS STJ> ),
```

set(
), set())

which is simply a list of sets separated by commas and surrounded by parentheses, and then find out which teams have remained in the Scottish premiership for all these years by applying the *reduction* operator

```
[∩] (set( <ABE CEL DUN HAM HEA INV KIL MOT PAR RAN ROS\
   STJ> ),
```

```
        set( <ABE CEL DUN DUU HAM HEA INV KIL MOT PAR ROS STJ> ),
        set(<ABE CEL DUN DUU HAM  INV KIL MOT PAR ROS STJ STM >)
        )
```

which will return a set of 10 teams that excludes Rangers, St. Mirren and Heart of Midlothian. But we have to think a bit to find that out. Set operators can also give us that information.

```
set( <ABE CEL DUN HAM HEA INV KIL MOT PAR RAN ROS STJ>\
    ) (^)
set( <ABE CEL DUN DUU HAM HEA INV KIL MOT PAR ROS STJ> )
```

will return the *symmetric difference* between the two sets, that is, the ones that are included in the first but not in the second and the other way round, in this case the two teams that were either demoted or promoted, which is this set: set(RAN, STM).

Picking fixtures out of this set is straightforward, using our well known pick:

```
set( <ABE CEL DUN HAM HEA INV KIL MOT PAR RAN ROS STJ>\
    ).pick(2)
```

If we wanted to randomly create a whole football day, we would have to keep eliminating teams in every fixture:

```
set( <ABE CEL DUN HAM HEA INV KIL MOT PAR RAN ROS STJ> ) (-)
set ( set( <ABE CEL DUN HAM HEA INV KIL MOT PAR RAN\
    ROS STJ> ).pick(2) )
```

where we *set-ize* the list returned by pick in order to take it away or substract from the original set.

Elements in a set

Which might be handy in cases such as this one

```
127 ∈  set(7,14...1000)
```

which is a very compact way of checking if 127 is, or not, multiple of seven and will return false, which means that

```
127 ∉  set(7,14...1000)
```

will obviously return `True`

Sets coming together

One cool things about sets is that you can use them as a single thing with several values at the same time. These are called Junctions [https://goo.gl/jSTkfg] and only match a single logical value if you evaluate them to return true or false.

```
all <innie minnie moe 0>
```

or

```
(so all <innie minnie moe Really>) == True
```

which uses `()` for grouping and `so`, as we have seen it before, to force a True or False value. In this case, the important part is the last element, `Really`, which makes it true or false.

But the useful thing about Junctions [https://goo.gl/GKfGEF] is how you can use them to check against several values at the same time; if you need to check something about several numbers at the same time, try this

```
so 84 == any 7,14…100
```

In this example, we are building a series with all multiples of 7 up to 100. `any` creates a Junction. The double equal sign will check 84 against all of the elements in the Junction, creating a new one that might have, or not, a True value. Applying `so` will return `True` as long as a single value is True. Obviously, `any` has an opposite: =none"

```
so 84 == none 11,22…100
```

will return `True`, since 84 does not appear to be a multiple of 11.

13

Secure connection

The whole point of programming is working with remote computers. And in fact it is almost impossible working nowadays without using several remote computers, *cloud* hosts as it were, to perform routine tasks. You need to connect to them, and do so efficiently and also securely. That is why *ssh* was invented. This is when you effectively notice that there is a lot of Internet above and beyond the web, and this is where we are going to start working with it.

Bear in mind that you do not need to use the cloud to need to connect securely to other computers. Something as routine as copying files from an old laptop to a new laptop can be done better and maybe even faster by connecting the two laptops to the local router and doing something like this:

```
rsync -avz -e ssh 192.168.1.38:/home/thisisme/ .
```

Let us suppose that you are thisisme and that, effectively, there is a ssh server running in the old laptop. What this command will do is to connect through your account to your old laptop, that is, become you there, and then start to copy all things from the old account to your new account, which is where you should be. This is much better than just doing a copy using 'cp' since you will effectively synchronize the two accounts; if there is something wrong along the line, you have to reset your router, whatever, you can start where you left it by issuing again the same command from the command line. But please bear in mind that what you have done here is first access a computer using its Internet protocol address, `192.168.1.38`, which is a local network address (usual routers start to assign addresses starting with 192.168.1.33) and proceed to *run* something, a copy order, in it.

You can in fact go a bit further and directly connect to it, provided you have been provided an account:

```
ssh thisisme@192.168.1.38
```

This will open a *shell* in that remote account, and you will be be able to run command line and console commands there. Even some windows-based commands, if the protocols have been configured correctly. But never mind that. Fact it you will be faced with a prompt, and whatever you run, `ls`, `emacs`, `perl`, whatever, will be run *there*, not at your own computer. You can even humor yourself and find out the computer you are connecting from (it will tell you something like `Last login: Sat Mar 18 11:19:42 2017 from 192.168.1.36`, this last one will be the IP address you are connecting *from* and connect *back* to your computer using that address. That is, provided ssh is running as a server and configured to allow this kind of connections.

It would be convenient to *not* use any other kind of connection. `ssh` means *secure shell*, and all traffic between the two computers (and back) is encrypted, that is, secured from prying eyes. But if you have to enter the password every time you will end up using a commons password, which goes against security. There is a way, however, to work without using a password. The procedure involves generating a *key pair*, that is, a pair of keys, a private key that will be secured in your computer, a public key that you will copy to the computer you are going to connect. The procedure is quite clearly explained in GitHub [https://goo.gl/r0PGlW] , but it goes basically like this:

```
ssh-keygen -t rsa -b 4096 -C "jjmerelo@gmail.com"
```

Use no passphrase, although you might have to use one if you are in a computer that lots of people can access. You will have something like this:

This is going to generate two files, a public and private key; the first

```
$ ssh-keygen -t rsa -b 4096 -C "jjmerelo@gmail.com"
Generating public/private rsa key pair.
Enter file in which to save the key (/home/jmerelo/.ssh/id_rsa):
Created directory '/home/jmerelo/.ssh'.
Enter passphrase (empty for no passphrase):
Enter same passphrase again:
Your identification has been saved in /home/jmerelo/.ssh/id_rsa.
Your public key has been saved in /home/jmerelo/.ssh/id_rsa.pub.
The key fingerprint is:
SHA256:NbtNNiRi0/Q5ZH8kmdzQYOjBVScQDH/g2fAH55obJlY jjmerelo@gmail.com
The key's randomart image is:
+---[RSA 4096]----+
|        o+B*OO=|
|       o *=X+B+|
|       + =.O.E +|
|      . + =.+ = |
|       S . * = |
|        * + o |
|       . . . |
|             |
|             |
+----[SHA256]-----+
```

Figure 13.1: Generating a key pair

one will have a .pub extension. That public key will be checked against your private one, but before you will have to copy it to the remote place

```
ssh-copy-id -i .ssh/id_rsa.pub thisisme@192.168.1.36
```

After which you will be able to connect directly to that address, without needing to do additional password-typing. Which will be extremely convenient for applications that need a fluid connection with no prompting.

14

Changing things

We have already seen how built-in functions operate on data and extract information from them or change them in different ways. In fact, operators such as * are nothing but functions in disguise, with 3 + 4 actually being actually `adds(3,4)`. Anything that operates or changes things, converting them into others, is a *function*, although if they use funny symbols we will call them operators.

It is going to be a lot of fun if we can build our own, right? Let's do exactly that.

```
{ $_ * 2 }
```

is a piece of code that will multiply by two whatever gets handled to it. The giveaway that turns it into a function are the curly brackets. Putting funny symbols that enclose, or close, other symbols has been used quite frequently, using quotes, or angle brackets, or parentheses to enclose arrays or lists or strings. The first giveaway here are those curly brackets. And the second is the $. Functions have to operate on something, right? So this $_ (dollar, underscore) will be a *stand-in* for whatever the function is going to operate in. In fact, you do not need this $_ to actually make a function; curly brackets are more than enough, but { 42 } would be a boring function that just returns the answer to life, the universe and everything. Let us find out how Perl6 calls these functions.

```
{ $_ * 2 }.^name
```

Will return **Block** which is what Perl6 calls these pieces of code that can act on other things and return stuff, like this

```
{ $_ * 2 }( 2 )
```

will apply the function to the number 2, returning, you guessed it, 4. Functions are applied to things using these parentheses, and, as you might have seen, $_ is a stand-in for whatever the function is called with, 2 in this case.

We have already seen a bit of these chunks of code in action previously, when using `grep`.

```
(1..1000).grep(* %% 11)
```

will return only numbers that are divisible by 11 by applying the function * %% 11, which returns **True** for every element that is divisible by 11 and forms a new list with all elements for which this expression is true. Instead of $_ as above we are using *, the wildcard symbol, which, of course, is called **Whatever** What we are using is, in fact, a *chunk of code* or **Block**, and in fact, we can rewrite the above expression this way:

```
(1..1000).grep( {$_ %% 11} )
```

showing that what we are doing it handling `grep` a block that returns a **True** or **False** value. There is still another way of doing it, because in Perl6, just like in Perl, there are many ways of doing everything:

```
(1..1000).grep: * %% 11
```

with the colon : opening the way for a block, a construction that is totally equivalent to the one above and saves a character (a visible character, anyway, because you will need the whitespace for legibility). This means that **Whatever**, that is, * and the *topical* variable, $_, can work in pretty much the same way. However, they cannot be used interchangeably. The curly block takes $_, while the colon or braced block takes *. This

```
(1..1000).grep($_ %% 11)
```

will positively end in an error. Besides, `Whatever` positively means whatever and you can use it for one or even several parameters. However, * * * is not the thing with the biggest readability ever.

Pointy blocks to the rescue. Pointy blocks [https://goo.gl/vzrtFX] have an arrow up front, and the arrow is followed by a list of parameter names:

```
(1..1000).grep: -> $a {$a %% 11}
```

This expression works exactly in the same as the rest of the expressions above (remember, there are many ways of doing it), provided that whatever is behind the arrow is also used as a variable inside the block in curly brackets. This is more verbose for this kind of expression, but it is even more verbose to write it this way, which is also equivalent:

```
(1..1000).grep: sub ($a) {$a %% 11}
```

Meet the `sub` keyword, which is used to name *subroutines*. What are subroutines? Actually, they are simply code blocks, and the fact that this code behaves the same as above is exactly for that reason. We have followed a path that takes us all the way from simple code chunks to *subroutines* or, as they are generally called, *functions*. Actually, our Blocks are basically subroutines with no name, except that subroutines, them too, can have no name, as above. However, they do have a *signature*, the list of parameters behind the arrow or the word `sub`, in parentheses in this case.

Blocks can be simpler than subroutines, however, so we do not even have to declare the names of those parameters. Use whatever you want, like here, as long as they have the dollar and caret in front:

```
{ $^foo ** $^bar }( 12,13 )
```

which will raise 12 to the 13th power; that is what ** does. We are using the oh so common foo and bar. In this case, the caret ^ is produced by typing the key wherever the caret is and then the space, since it is a key that is usually composed as a circumflex accent with other characters to produce things like *brûlé*, which looks like it has been made up by some word inventor, but is actually French.

And while But do you remember that Perl 6 can easily deal with Unicode characters? From now on I propose to use ß and þ as substitutes for the hackneyed `foo` and `bar`, like here

```
{ ([*] 1..$^ß ) / ( [*] 1..$^þ) * ([*] 1..($^ß - $^þ))\
  }(5,3)
```

the part between braces computes n over m, that is, the binomial coefficient [https://goo.gl/8ws8Mc] . It does so by computing the factorial of ß, which is what `[*] 1..$^ß` does, remember, the meta-operator `[]` applied to `*` applies the product to all the elements in the range 1:ß. And then it divides it by the factorial of þ multiplied by the factorial of ß - þ. Easy, right? Remember not to use too big numbers, or it will take a little while.

You actually have to use these placeholders if you want to build up stuff using these chunks of code:

```
( { $^ß * 2},{$^þ / 2} )
```

is an array of code blocks. The same thing with `$_` would yield a rather weird error related to something being *raw*, but they are placeholders all the same. And what do we have here? A little list of code blocks. Before we have applied single code blocks to arrays of non-code things. But code things are also things, or, as it is said it functional programming, they are first-class citizens, so you can apply code blocks to code blocks, like here:

```
( { $^ß * 2},{$^þ / 2} ).grep:  { $_.(2) %% 2 }
```

Try to wrap your head around this, which is functional programming in a nutshell. Remember how `$_` was used as a placeholder for things like numbers before? We are using it here as a placeholder for code blocks. So what `$_.(2)` does is to apply (herein the `.()`) code block to the number two, and then apply the *divisible by* operator `%%`. Eventually, it will be true if the code block, applied to the number two, returns something that is divisible by two. In this case, it will return an array with a single element, the first one in the array, obviously. Once again, check this out, because it is quite cool. Not cool as in can't-be-done-in-any-other-language, but still cool: we have applied a function to a list of functions which returns another list of functions.

So these are functions for you. In Perl 6.

Going back to sequences

As we always do in this book, we will try to apply what we know to defining and creating sequences; there are lots of them [https://goo.gl/Y7nXrn] than can be used for fun and enlightenment.

These expressions allow us to be much more flexible when building sequences, which, as it happens, are becoming a showcase of Perl 6 power and features. For starters, these chunks of code can be used to generate new sequences from old ones

```
map *², 1..∞
```

This expression, that uses `map` for the first time, is the sequence of all square natural numbers. `map` effectively *maps*, as in a function, one value to another, creating a new element out of the old elements of the array it maps via an expression. And the code chunk we use for mapping is `*²`, which elevates to the second power `Whatever`. If you want to see it in a more code-like form,

```
(map {$^þ²}, 1..∞)[333]
```

which uses the placeholder `$^þ` instead of `Whatever` and, since it is now a proper chunk of code, it has to be surrounded by curly braces. Besides, we are using the result, which is an infinite sequence, as a real object of which we extract element number 333. We can use whatever element we want, since it is infinite, and this is, besides, a way of holding in a lazy sequence all integer squares *in the world*. Besides, this is a map as in a real function: defined from an infinite set onto another infinite set. Mind you, it is not a `Set`, just a set in the general sense. `Sets` are finite, sets are not.

You can also use these expressions to define series where new elements are the result of applying some operation to the former elements. See it here:

```
(1,.9999999999999999, { $^ß * $^þ}...∞)
```

This is a theoretically infinite series, which, in fact, goes to 0 pretty fast due to the actually finite nature of real numbers as represented by computers, and where each term is the result of multiplying the two previous terms. Just try and find out the 100 first terms and you will see that beyond the first 90 it is actually not so far away from 0. You know, sequences can converge or, actually, diverge.

Divergence is not actually a big deal. The whole idea of the Mandelbrot set [https://goo.gl/Wm5ZQF] is built around it. Apply z²+c to any number c and see what happens. Does it diverge? It's not in the Mandelbrot set. Does it not? Well, assign it a beautiful color and draw it. We do it right here:

```
(0,{$^ß²+0.5+0.3i}...∞)[^100]
```

Which is a sequence just like the old ones, only it's got an i. Well, we were before talking about a number c and that is is because it is a *complex* number. Complex numbers are pairs of *real* numbers, where one part of the couple is called real and the other, the one that precedes i, *imaginary*. Just think about them like your old x and y numbers, only i² is equal to -1, so when we elevate complex numbers to the second power, they can sometimes turn into real numbers. No big deal, really; the big deal is that what we have above is a series of complex numbers which will actually diverge to a Inf-Inf i value, which is how Perl represents a couple of infinites. But not all values go to infinity.

```
(0,{$^ß²-0.5+0.3i}...∞)[^100]
```

Precisely at the other side of the *real* axis, this value will never go to infinity; if you look at the mandelbrot set, it would be to the left and top of the toppled heart-like shape, in the black area; actually, it converges to something like -0.382545950491141+0.169962816621862i after a few iterations. The whole point of this is to show how, using just a simple expression, you can define complex mathematical relations and sequences. With Perl 6, of course.

Besides, remember, functions are first class citizens, and sequences two. You can create a code chunk that returns a sequence, and combine placeholders to do so. Check this out:

```
{ (0,{$^ß²+$_}...∞) }
```

This is a code chunk that returns a sequence; the only thing we have done is to put curly brackets around it. We have two different kind of placeholders: $_ will be a stand-in for whatever we handle to the code chunk, while $ß is the placeholder for the sequence itself. Perl 6 is able to find out which is which. And sequence generators generate sequences:

```
{ (0,{$^ß²+$_}...∞) }(.01+.1i)
```

Here we use parenthesis to hand the number that will substitute $_ in the sequence. And, of course, we can also use the infinite sequence itself via a couple of more parentheses:

```
({ (0,{$^ß²+$_}...∞) }(.01+.1i))[^100]
```

These last parentheses wrap around the sequence so that we can get the range of its first 100 elements. Being as it is in the middle of the belly of the set, it converges.

15

Errors are not errors

Shit eventually happens. But when it does, you should know that it is not really shit, but a brown and maybe a bit smelly thing, and that anyway you must be ready to unshit everything, because shit cannot be ignored by starting all over again. The first thing that you have to understand is that errors are your friends. 80 years of computer science have eventually given us systems and languages that, when something unexpected happens, explain quite well what's the problem and even hint at what can be done to fix it. Not go all the way to fix it, because that is actually why errors happen, because the interpreter (in this case) or the system (in general) cannot quite figure out what you mean and tell you in about so many words. Maybe more.

Besides, error is too strong a word. You see errors, and you think of failure, as in *You are a*. That's not quite it. Errors in computers, and even more so in computer languages, are actually misunderstandings, and always a path to eventually get things right. They are a way of saying /You are probably right, but could you please explain things in a slightly different way so that I can actually confirm that?/

Let us see an example. Say that you skip a curly bracket, like this

```
( { $^ß * 2},{$^þ / 2 )
```

Happens all the time, right? You skip a key, maybe avert your gaze to check out incoming Telegram messages, whatever. And then that happens. The interpreter will tell you this:

```
> ( { $^ß * 2},{$^þ / 2 )
( { $^ß * 2},{$^þ / 2 )
===SORRY!=== Error while compiling:
Missing block
------> ( { $^ß * 2},{$^þ / 2 ⏏
    expecting any of:
        statement end
        statement modifier
        statement modifier loop
```

Figure 15.1: Errored expression in the REPL

First is says what's wrong. `Missing block`. It is not as helpful as, "Hey, you forgot to put curly braces here", but, once again, if it would have been able to figure that out it would have fixed it by itself. But you can work with that error. If you cannot really point out what's wrong, Google is your friend [https://goo.gl/4D7JjP] , and will take you to this article of Zoffix Znet on, precisely, Perl 6 errors [https://goo.gl/XcG2vp] . That example points out to the fact that Perl 6 says so when it is waiting for some block to be there, or, as it happens here, to be properly enclosed. Besides, the next line is even more helpful, pointing out with a yellow   exactly the place where it should have been whatever it was expecting, a curly bracket in this case. See? It has been just a misunderstanding. Besides, it is much clearer later on. It is saying it was expecting either an statement end, or modifier, or modifier loop. The } is how you put an end to the block. The fact that there are three different things is the reason why the error, let's not call it error any more, the misunderstanding, is there in the first place. There were three possible things that could go there, and poor Perl 6 cannot understand which one you meant. It is no big deal, really, but you see how reading the error carefully will help you find the solution fast enough.

All misunderstandings in Perl 6 will follow the same structure. First, the error, what is wrong. Second, where it is wrong, and third, what it was expecting, and also the reason why it really could not recover from the error.

Some errors will not arrive from typing, but from applying what you know of other languages here.

```
( 3 == 2)?"Yes":"No"
```

This ternary operator is not going to work here. However, there is a very helpful error message

Figure 15.2: Helpful error message

In this case, it is perfectly clear to Camelia, the friendly Perl6 interpreter, what's wrong. However, the problem is that in this new Perl6 language it simply cannot be done that way, so it says in Perl 6 please use ?? and !!. You see? Not only I understand you, but take you by the hand to the use of features that are almost, but not quite, the same as you did before.

Misunderstandings will happen here, there and everywhere. So it is better not to make a big fuss about them. Check them out carefully, try to follow the advice, if any, check out DuckDuckGo or Google for possible solutions, and, if everything fails, you can still try and get some help from the community. We will see to that later on.

Worse errors are those in which the computer actually does something, but not really what you were looking for.

16

Where did I put my keys?

Vectors and sequences are nice ways of arranging things, one after the other, but they are just a simple way of getting to a particular value in a bunch of things. One value is stored in the first position (which, remember, is always referred to as 0), and another in the position 333. The language takes care of doing some computation to access whatever is stored in position 333. At the end of the day, you use a *key*, which happens to be a number, to compute the place where the corresponding value is stored, but sequences are simply lists of pairs with position and the value stored in that position.

But think about hotel rooms. They do not go all the way from 0 to the total number of rooms, they use some code that starts with the floor number and that continues with some sequence of numbers in the floor. If you used a series to name the rooms or to say how many persons were there in each room, many rooms would be *void* because simply they would not exists. There is another way, however. Let us say we have this little cute boutique hotel with four rooms. Every room will have a name, a maximum capability, and an *amenities* list. Every room will have something like this

```
name: Lilly
PAX: 3
amenities: Boiler, Fan, barely any spider
```

Programming languages have different structures to hold different types of data. What we are looking for here is some kind of structure that allows you to access information by *key*. If I somehow get hold of the room, asking about the name will return the name the room has been given.

Let's try this

```
{ name => 'Lilly', PAX => 3, amenities => 'Boiler,\
  Fan, barely any spider'}
```

which would define pretty much what we have above. If we say:

```
{ name => 'Lilly', PAX => 3, amenities => 'Boiler,\
  Fan, barely any spider'}<name>
```

or

```
{ name => 'Lilly', PAX => 3, amenities => 'Boiler,\
  Fan, barely any spider'}{"name"}
```

we will get the name of the room we are dealing with. Once again the angular things <> serve as a shortcut to avoid using quotes, which we can use if we want, as in the second example. Say we are not interested in the amenities. We can extract a part of the values so:

```
{ name => 'Lilly', PAX => 3, amenities => 'Boiler,\
  Fan, barely any spider'}<name PAX>
```

But this a single room, and we need the whole hotel. Let's do it here:

```
{
  101 => {
     PAX => 3,
     amenities => "Boiler, Fan, barely any spider",
     name => "Lilly"
  },
  102 => {
     PAX => 1,
     amenities => "Open air, no ceiling",
```

```
        name => "Daffodil"
    },
    201 => {
        PAX => 2,
        amenities => "IKEA room, build it your way",
        name => "Rose"
    }
}
```

Can we access how the amenities of a single room? Sure:

```
{
    101 => {
        PAX => 3,
        amenities => "Boiler, Fan, barely any spider",
        name => "Lilly"
    },
    102 => {
        PAX => 1,
        amenities => "Open air, no ceiling",
        name => "Daffodil"
    },
    201 => {
        PAX => 2,
        amenities => "IKEA room, build it your way",
        name => "Rose"
    }
}<101><amenities>
```

There is however no way of telling which ones are occupied. We can use a logical value to do so, this way:

```
{
    101 => {
        PAX => 3,
        amenities => "Boiler, Fan, barely any spider",
        name => "Lilly",
        :occupied
    },
    102 => {
```

```
      PAX => 1,
      amenities => "Open air, no ceiling",
      name => "Daffodil"
   },
   201 => {
      PAX => 2,
      amenities => "IKEA room, build it your way",
      name => "Rose",
      :occupied
   }
}
```

When you type this, you will see that :occupied is translated as

```
occupied => True
```

The colon : in front of the key *turns on* that value, making it a key whose value is true; it does double duty: creates a key-value pair, and also gives it a true value. What about the "False" value? Nothing: if it is not there, it could as well be false.

And things are getting a bit complicated here to type them all over again. We are going to need to give things a name pretty soon.

www.ingramcontent.com/pod-product-compliance
Lightning Source LLC
Chambersburg PA
CBHW031247050326
40690CB00007B/995